DOG BREEDS

GOLDENDOODLES

BY LIBBY WILSON

WWW.APEXEDITIONS.COM

Copyright © 2025 by Apex Editions, Mendota Heights, MN 55120. All rights reserved. No part of this book may be reproduced or utilized in any form or by any means without written permission from the publisher.

Apex is distributed by North Star Editions:
sales@northstareditions.com | 888-417-0195

Produced for Apex by Red Line Editorial.

Photographs ©: iStockphoto, cover, 6, 7, 8–9, 20, 25; Shutterstock Images, 1, 12–13, 14, 15, 16–17, 18–19, 21, 22–23, 24, 27, 29; Mike Wolanin/The Republic/AP Images, 4–5; Chris Boswell/Alamy, 10–11

Library of Congress Control Number: 2023921790

ISBN
978-1-63738-910-2 (hardcover)
978-1-63738-950-8 (paperback)
979-8-89250-047-0 (ebook pdf)
979-8-89250-008-1 (hosted ebook)

Printed in the United States of America
Mankato, MN
082024

NOTE TO PARENTS AND EDUCATORS

Apex books are designed to build literacy skills in striving readers. Exciting, high-interest content attracts and holds readers' attention. The text is carefully leveled to allow students to achieve success quickly. Additional features, such as bolded glossary words for difficult terms, help build comprehension.

TABLE OF CONTENTS

CHAPTER 1
FURRY FRIEND 4

CHAPTER 2
HYBRID DOGS 10

CHAPTER 3
DIFFERENT LOOKS 16

CHAPTER 4
GOLDENDOODLE CARE 22

COMPREHENSION QUESTIONS • 28
GLOSSARY • 30
TO LEARN MORE • 31
ABOUT THE AUTHOR • 31
INDEX • 32

CHAPTER 1

FURRY FRIEND

A goldendoodle walks through the halls of a hospital. Her name is Agnes. She is a **therapy** dog. Today, she is visiting **patients**.

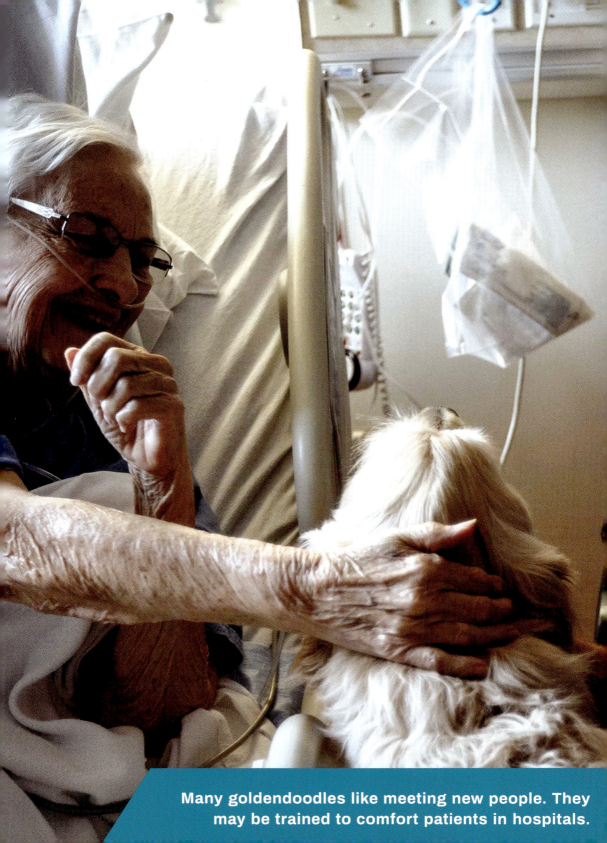

Many goldendoodles like meeting new people. They may be trained to comfort patients in hospitals.

Therapy dogs can show patients that checkups are not scary.

Agnes goes to several children's rooms. The children are sick or hurt. Some feel scared. But their faces light up when Agnes walks in. The friendly dog calms their fears.

TRAINING

All therapy dogs go through training. The dogs learn to stay calm and move slowly. They get used to new noises and smells. That way, they can help people stay calm, too.

Some therapy dogs visit schools. They sit with students as they read.

The children pet and cuddle Agnes. Some nap with her in their beds. Others play with Agnes. Everyone is happier after seeing her.

FAST FACT

Therapy dogs help some patients get exercise. Dogs and patients walk or play with toys.

Walking with a therapy dog can help patients get stronger.

CHAPTER 2

Hybrid Dogs

Goldendoodles are hybrid dogs. This means they are a mix of two **breeds**. One breed is the golden **retriever**. The other is the poodle.

Poodles and golden retrievers are both known for being smart dogs.

Goldendoodles get some traits from poodles and some traits from golden retrievers.

Many breeders began mixing the two breeds in the 1990s. They wanted the golden retriever's sweet **personality**. But they wanted the poodle's low-shedding coat.

LESS SHEDDING

Many people are **allergic** to dogs. Dogs that shed less are easier for these people to be around. Many doodles **inherit** low-shedding coats from their parents. But some doodles still shed.

The hybrid dogs quickly became popular. People began creating different sizes. They used standard, miniature, and toy poodles. They bred large, medium, and small doodles.

Standard poodles are large dogs. Toy poodles are tiny.

Labradoodles are a cross of poodles and Labrador retrievers.

FAST FACT

Labradoodles and cockapoos are other poodle hybrids.

CHAPTER 3

Different Looks

Because doodles are hybrids, their looks can vary quite a bit. Fur is one example. Many goldendoodles have curly coats. But some have straight or wavy fur.

Goldendoodles with curly coats tend to shed less.

Many doodles have golden fur. But doodles can also be white, black, or brown.

Goldendoodles come in many colors. Their size can vary, too. It depends on the type of poodle they were bred from.

PARTI PATTERNS

Some doodles' coats have patterns. Parti coats are one example. In this pattern, fur is at least half white. It has patches of another solid color.

Standard goldendoodles are more than 21 inches (53 cm) high at the shoulders.

FAST FACT

Most goldendoodles live 10 to 15 years.

Doodles bred from standard poodles are large. They can weigh up to 90 pounds (41 kg). The smallest doodles come from toy poodles. They can weigh less than 25 pounds (11 kg).

Miniature goldendoodles are less than 17 inches (43 cm) high at the shoulders.

CHAPTER 4

GOLDENDOODLE CARE

Goldendoodles are active dogs. They need to exercise every day. Large doodles need lots of room to run.

Goldendoodles should get 30 to 60 minutes of exercise each day.

If left alone, doodles can become stressed or make messes.

Doodles also need lots of **attention**. They shouldn't be left alone very long. They may bark or dig. Doodles need training, too. They are eager to please and learn tricks quickly.

FAST FACT
Most doodles get along well with children and other pets.

Doodles are easy to train. But it's important to start when they are puppies.

HEALTH TESTS

Most doodles are healthy. But some inherit diseases from their parents. People can buy dogs from breeders who use health tests. These tests make sure dogs and their puppies aren't at risk.

A goldendoodle's curly hair **mats** easily. So, grooming is important. Dogs should be brushed daily. They also need haircuts every couple of months.

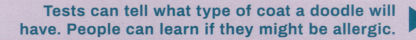

Tests can tell what type of coat a doodle will have. People can learn if they might be allergic.

COMPREHENSION QUESTIONS

Write your answers on a separate piece of paper.

1. Write a few sentences explaining the main ideas of Chapter 2.

2. Would you want to own a goldendoodle? Why or why not?

3. How much do goldendoodles shed?
   - A. No goldendoodles shed at all.
   - B. All goldendoodles shed a lot.
   - C. Many goldendoodles don't shed much.

4. Why don't all goldendoodles look the same?
   - A. Each dog has some poodle traits and some golden traits.
   - B. Each dog is mix of three different breeds.
   - C. Goldendoodles were not bred on purpose.

5. What does **vary** mean in this book?

*Goldendoodles come in many colors. Their size can **vary**, too.*

- **A.** be all the same
- **B.** be different
- **C.** be made up

6. What does **grooming** mean in this book?

*A goldendoodle's curly hair mats easily. So, **grooming** is important. Dogs should be brushed daily.*

- **A.** giving an animal its food
- **B.** caring for an animal's fur
- **C.** keeping an animal outdoors

Answer key on page 32.

GLOSSARY

allergic
Reacting to something by feeling sick.

attention
Time spent with a person or animal.

breeds
Specific types of dogs that have their own looks and abilities.

inherit
To have something be passed down from parents.

mats
Forms thick, tangled clumps.

patients
People who receive medical care.

personality
The way a person or animal usually acts.

retriever
A type of dog bred to find and bring back animals during hunts.

therapy
Treatment that helps with healing.

TO LEARN MORE

BOOKS

Earley, Christina. *Goldendoodles*. Coral Springs, FL: Seahorse Publishing, 2022.

Lilley, Matt. *Therapy Dogs*. Mendota Heights, MN: Apex Editions, 2023.

Pearson, Marie. *Dogs*. Mankato, MN: The Child's World, 2021.

ONLINE RESOURCES

Visit **www.apexeditions.com** to find links and resources related to this title.

ABOUT THE AUTHOR

Libby Wilson has loved books and reading her entire life. She enjoys researching and finding interesting facts to share with readers. Her favorite topics are nature, history, and inspirational people. For the past 11 years, Ms. Wilson has been owned by Molly, the world's sweetest golden retriever.

INDEX

C
coat, 13, 16
colors, 18–19

E
exercise, 22

G
golden retrievers, 10, 13
grooming, 26

H
health tests, 26
hybrid dogs, 10, 13–15, 16

M
miniature poodles, 14

P
poodles, 10, 13–15, 18, 21

S
shedding, 13
sizes, 14, 18
standard poodles, 14, 21

T
therapy dogs, 4, 6, 8
toy poodles, 14, 21
training, 7, 24

W
weight, 21

ANSWER KEY:
1. Answers will vary; 2. Answers will vary; 3. C; 4. A; 5. B; 6. B